A Picture Book of the Mass

Presented To:

_____

By:

_____

On:

_____

The Good Shepherd, Philippe de Champaigne

INTRODUCTORY RITES

Entrance

Stand

As the priest enters the church, a processional hymn or chant may be sung.

Song of the Angels,
William Bouguereau

Greeting

Priest: **In the name of the Father, and of the Son, and of the Holy Spirit.**
People: **Amen.**
Priest: **The Lord be with you.**
People: **And with your spirit.**

Penitential Act

*The priest calls upon the congregation
to join together to confess our sins
and celebrate God's mercy.*

I confess to almighty God
and to you my brothers and sisters,
that I have greatly sinned,
in my thoughts and in my words,
in what I have done
and in what I have failed to do,

{ through my fault, through my fault,
through my most grievous fault; } *(strike breast)*

therefore I ask blessed Mary ever-Virgin,
all the Angels and Saints,
and you, my brothers and sisters,
to pray for me to the Lord our God.

Penitent Magdalene, Guido Reni

OR:

Priest:
Have mercy on us, O Lord.

People:
For we have sinned against you.

Priest:
Show us, O Lord, your mercy.

People:
And grant us your salvation.

Divine Mercy,
Eugene Kazimierowski

Kyrie

Priest: Lord, have mercy.
People: Lord, have mercy.
Priest: Christ, have mercy.
People: Christ, have mercy.
Priest: Lord, have mercy.
People: Lord, have mercy.

In Greek, this is "Kyrie, eleison. Christe, eleison. Kyrie, eleison."

Gloria

Adoration of the Shepherds,
Unknown German Artist

Glory to God in the highest,
and on earth peace to people of good will.

We praise you,
we bless you,
we adore you,
we glorify you,
we give you thanks for your great glory,
Lord God, heavenly King,
O God, almighty Father.

Lord Jesus Christ, Only Begotten Son,
Lord God, Lamb of God, Son of the Father,
you take away the sins of the world,
    have mercy on us;
you take away the sins of the world,
    receive our prayer;
you are seated at the right hand of the Father,
    have mercy on us.

For you alone are the Holy One,
you alone are the Lord,
you alone are the Most High,
Jesus Christ,
with the Holy Spirit,
in the glory of God the Father.
Amen.

THE LITURGY OF THE WORD

First Reading

This reading is usually taken from the Old Testament. At the end of the reading:

Lector: **The word of the Lord.**
People: **Thanks be to God.**

Moses Receives the Tablets of the Law, Joao Zeferino da Costa

Responsorial Psalm

A Psalm follows the first reading to encourage meditation on the Word of God. The congregation is led in singing or saying the refrain.

David Playing the Harp, Gerrit van Honthorst

Second Reading

This reading is usually taken from the New Testament letters. At the end of the reading:

Lector:
The word of the Lord.
People:
Thanks be to God.

Apostle Paul, Rembrandt van Rijn

Gospel Acclamation

Stand

The congregation rises, sings "Alleluia," and prepares to hear the message of the Gospel.

People: Alleluia.

Gospel

The Four Evangelists, Abraham Bloemaert

Priest or Deacon: **The Lord be with you.**
People: **And with your spirit.**
Priest or Deacon: **A reading from the holy Gospel according to _____.**
People: **Glory to you, O Lord.**

Use your thumb to make a cross on your forehead, lips, and heart, while reflecting: "May the Gospel be in my mind, on my lips, and in my heart."

At the conclusion of the Gospel:

Priest or Deacon: **The Gospel of the Lord.**
People: **Praise to you, Lord Jesus Christ.**

Homily

The priest teaches us about the readings we have heard, and helps us to understand our faith and apply God's Word to our own lives.

Sermon on the Mount, Carl Heinrick Bloch

Profession of Faith

Stand

The congregation joins together to recite the Nicene Creed, which is a statement of our beliefs.

> I believe in one God,
> the Father almighty,
> maker of heaven and earth,
> of all things visible and invisible.
> I believe in one Lord Jesus Christ,
> the Only Begotten Son of God,
> born of the Father before all ages.

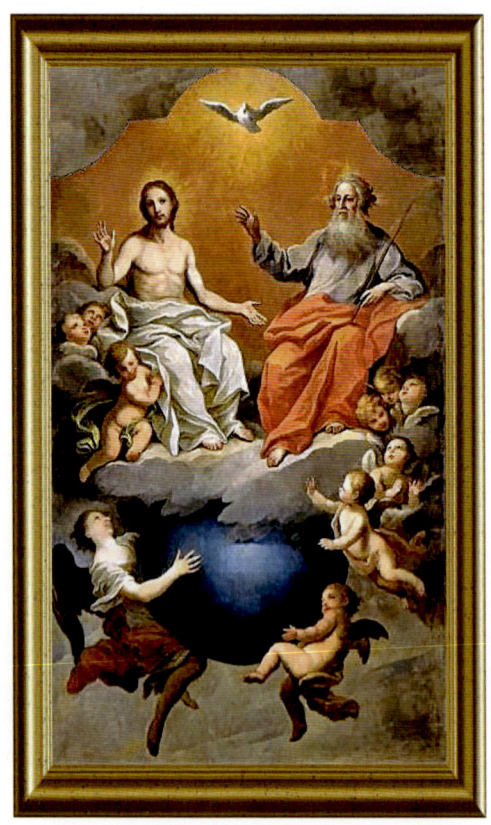

Holy Trinity, Szymon Czechowicz

God from God, Light from Light,
true God from true God,
begotten, not made,
    consubstantial with the Father;
through him all things were made.
For us men and for our salvation
he came down from heaven,

{ and by the Holy Spirit was incarnate
    of the Virgin Mary,
and became man. } *(bow during these words)*

For our sake he was crucified
    under Pontius Pilate,
he suffered death and was buried,
and rose again on the third day
in accordance with the Scriptures.
He ascended into heaven
and is seated at the right hand of the Father.
He will come again in glory
to judge the living and the dead
and his kingdom will have no end.

The Last Judgment, Fra Angelico

I believe in the Holy Spirit, the Lord,
    the giver of life,
who proceeds from the Father and the Son,
who with the Father and the Son
    is adored and glorified,
who has spoken through the prophets.

I believe in one, holy, catholic and
    apostolic Church.
I confess one Baptism for the forgiveness of sins
and I look forward to the resurrection
    of the dead
and the life of the world to come. Amen.

Resurrection of Christ, Carl Heinrick Bloch

Prayer of the Faithful

Together we offer general intercessions, including those for the needs of the Church, for the poor and suffering, and for the salvation of the world.
After each intention:

Leader: We pray to the Lord.
People: Lord, hear our prayer.

THE LITURGY OF THE EUCHARIST

The Last Supper, Juan de Juanes

Preparation of the Gifts

As a hymn or chant is sung, the congregation has the opportunity to make an offering. The gifts of bread and wine are brought to the altar along with the offerings of the people.

Fresco in Basilica of St. Martin (Wurttenberg)

Priest: Blessed are you, Lord God of all creation, for through your goodness we have received the bread we offer to you: fruit of the earth and work of human hands, it will become for us the bread of life.

People: Blessed be God forever.

The Emmaus Disciples, Abraham Bloemaert

The Virgin Adoring the Host,
Jean Augustine Dominique Ingres

Priest: Blessed are you, Lord God of all creation, for through your goodness we have received the wine we offer you: fruit of the vine and work of human hands, it will become our spiritual drink.

People: Blessed be God forever.

Invitation to Prayer

Priest: Pray, brethren, that my sacrifice and yours may be acceptable to God, the almighty Father.

People: May the Lord accept the sacrifice at your hands for the praise and glory of his name, for our good and the good of all his holy Church.

Stand

Prayer Over the Offerings

*The priest says a prayer over the gifts,
to which we respond:*

People: **Amen.**

Eucharistic Prayer

Priest: **The Lord be with you.**
People: **And with your spirit.**
Priest: **Lift up your hearts.**
People: **We lift them up to the Lord.**
Priest: **Let us give thanks to the Lord our God.**
People: **It is right and just.**

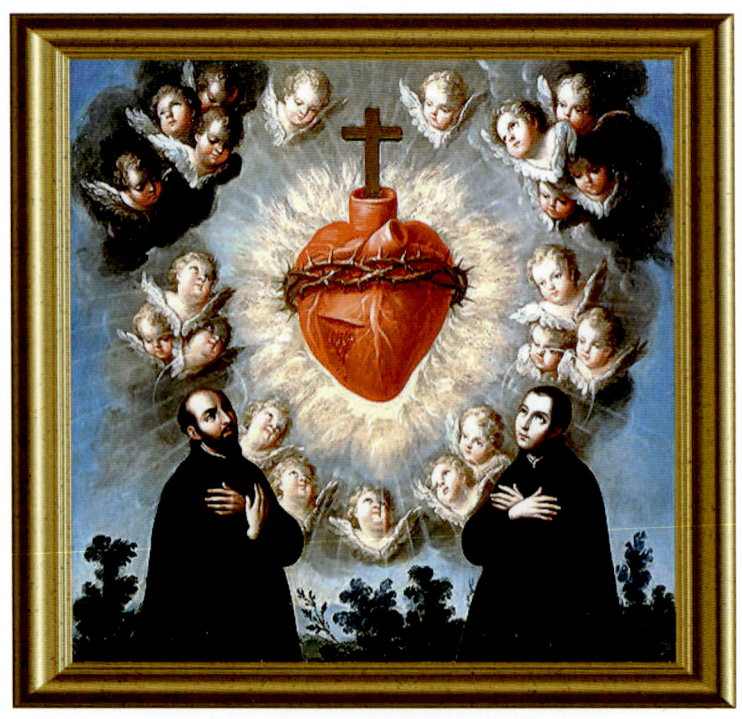

Sacred Heart of Jesus with St. Ignatius and St. Louis,
José de Páez

The Sanctus

We praise God in union with the Angels.

*Christ Surrounded by Musician Angels.
Altarpiece of Santa Maria la Real de Nájera.*

**Holy, Holy, Holy Lord God of hosts.
Heaven and earth are full of your glory.
Hosanna in the highest.
Blessed is he who comes in the
name of the Lord.
Hosanna in the highest.**

Kneel

Entry of Christ into Jerusalem, Santi Tito

Words of the Institution

During the Consecration, the bread and wine truly become the Body and Blood of Jesus. The priest may choose different versions of the Eucharistic Prayer.

Priest: At the time he was betrayed and entered willingly into his Passion, he took bread and, giving thanks, broke it, and gave it to his disciples, saying:

TAKE THIS, ALL OF YOU, AND EAT OF IT, FOR THIS IS MY BODY, WHICH WILL BE GIVEN UP FOR YOU.

Christ with the Eucharist, Vicente Juan Masip

The Last Supper, Leonardo da Vinci

Priest: In a similar way, when supper was ended, he took the chalice and, once more giving thanks, he gave it to his disciples, saying:

Take this, all of you, and drink from it, for this is the chalice of my Blood, the Blood of the new and eternal covenant, which will be poured out for you and for many for the forgiveness of sins. Do this in memory of me.

The Wedding Feast at Cana, Julius Carolsfeld

23

The Mystery of Faith

Priest: The mystery of faith.
People: We proclaim your Death, O Lord, and profess your Resurrection until you come again.

Or: When we eat this Bread and drink this Cup, we proclaim your Death, O Lord, until you come again.

Or: Save us, Savior of the world, for by your Cross and Resurrection, you have set us free.

Tryptich of the Blood of Christ

Great Amen

Priest: Through him and with him, and in him, O God, almighty Father, in the unity of the Holy Spirit, all glory and honor is yours, for ever and ever.
People: Amen. *(This response may be sung.)*

Communion Rite

We pray the Lord's Prayer together:

Stand

Our Father, who art in heaven,
hallowed be thy name;
thy kingdom come,
thy will be done
on earth as it is in heaven.
Give us this day our daily bread,
and forgive us our trespasses,
as we forgive those who trespass against us;
and lead us not into temptation,
but deliver us from evil.

Priest: Deliver us, Lord, we pray, from every evil, graciously grant peace in our days, that, by the help of your mercy, we may be always free from sin and safe from all distress, as we await the blessed hope and the coming of our Savior, Jesus Christ.

People: For the kingdom, the power and the glory are yours, now and for ever.

The Lord's Prayer,
James Joseph Jacques Tissot

Sign of Peace

The priest says a prayer, then the congregation offers each other a sign of peace.

Priest: **The peace of the Lord be with you always.**
People: **And with your spirit.**
Priest: **Let us offer each other the sign of peace.**

Now you may turn to the people around you and say, "Peace be with you."

Jesus with the Children, Marie Ellenrieder

Breaking of the Bread

Lamb of God, you take away the sins of the world, have mercy on us.

Lamb of God, you take away the sins of the world, have mercy on us.

Lamb of God, you take away the sins of the world, grant us peace.

Invitation to Communion

Kneel

Priest: Behold the Lamb of God, behold him who takes away the sins of the world. Blessed are those called to the supper of the Lamb.

Adoration of the Lamb, Jan van Eyck

People: Lord, I am not worthy that you should enter under my roof, but only say the word and my soul shall be healed.

Healing the Centurion's Servant, Paolo Veronese

We Receive Communion

All Catholics who have made their First Communion and are in a state of grace may now receive the Eucharist.

Priest:	**Priest:**
The Body of Christ.	**The Blood of Christ.**
Communicant: Amen.	**Communicant: Amen.**

Communion of the Apostles, San Marco

Period of Silence or Song of Praise

Kneel

Kneel and pray a prayer of thanksgiving in silence; then you may join in singing.

Prayer After Communion

Priest: **Let us pray.**

The priest says a special prayer, and when he is finished he says:

Stand

Priest: **Through Christ our Lord.**
People: **Amen.**

CONCLUDING RITES

Priest: **The Lord be with you.**
People: **And with your spirit.**
Priest: **May almighty God bless you, the Father, the Son, and the Holy Spirit.**
People: **Amen.**

The priest tells us to go in peace.

People: **Thanks be to God.**

A recessional song may be sung as the priest exits.

Predella of the San Domenico Altarpiece, Fra Angelico

Apostles Creed

I believe in God, the Father almighty, Creator of heaven and earth, and in Jesus Christ, his only Son, our Lord, who was conceived by the Holy Spirit, born of the Virgin Mary, suffered under Pontius Pilate, was crucified, died, and was buried; he descended into hell; on the third day he rose again from the dead; he ascended into heaven, and is seated at the right hand of God the Father almighty; from there he will come to judge the living and the dead. I believe in the Holy Spirit, the holy catholic Church, the communion of saints, the forgiveness of sins, the resurrection of the body, and life everlasting. Amen.